BEGINNING FOLK FOR PIANO

Boston Music Company
part of The Music Sales Group
London / New York / Paris / Sydney / Copenhagen / Berlin / Madrid / Tokyo

Published by
Boston Music Company
257 Park Avenue South, New York, NY10010, USA.

Exclusive Distributors:
Music Sales Corporation
257 Park Avenue South, New York, NY10010, USA.
Music Sales Limited
Distribution Centre, Newmarket Road,
Bury St Edmunds, Suffolk IP33 3YB, UK.
Music Sales Pty Limited
120 Rothschild Avenue,
Rosebery, NSW 2018, Australia.

Order No. BMC-12485
ISBN 978-1-84772-370-3

This book © Copyright 2007
Boston Music Company
a division of Music Sales Limited.

Music edited by Sam Harrop.
Cover design by Michael Bell Design.
Printed in the United States of America.

Your Guarantee of Quality
As publishers, we strive to produce every book to the highest commercial standards.
This book has been carefully designed to minimize awkward page turns and
to make playing from it a real pleasure.
Particular care has been given to specifying acid-free, neutral-sized paper made from
pulps which have not been elemental chlorine bleached.
This pulp is from farmed sustainable forests and was produced with special regard for the environment.
Throughout, the printing and binding have been planned to ensure a sturdy,
attractive publication which should give years of enjoyment.
If your copy fails to meet our high standards, please inform us and we will gladly replace it.

www.musicsales.com

All The Pretty Little Horses

Traditional American Folk Song

The Ash Grove

Traditional Welsh Folk Song

Barbara Allen

Traditional British Folk Song

The British Grenadiers

Traditional British Marching Song

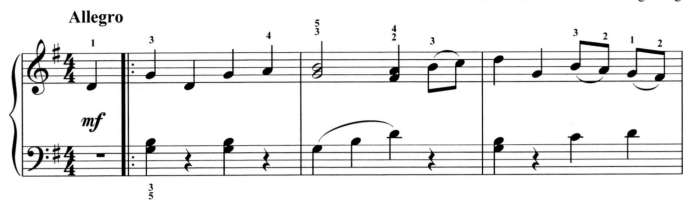

Down By The Sally Gardens

Traditional Irish Folk Song

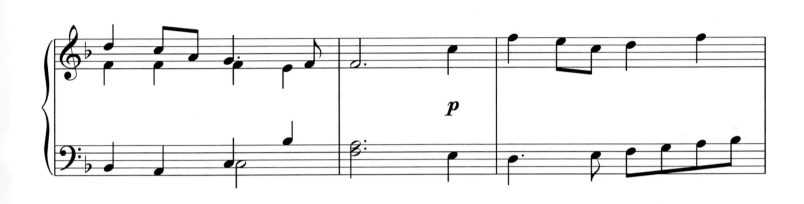

poco rit.   a tempo

English Country Garden

Traditional English Folk Song

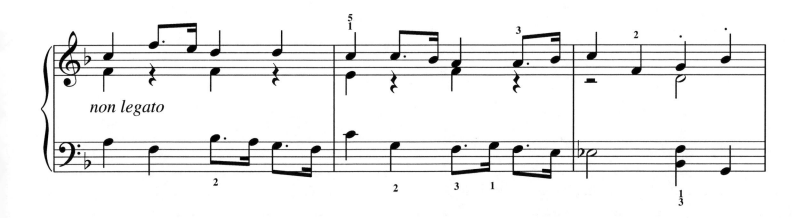

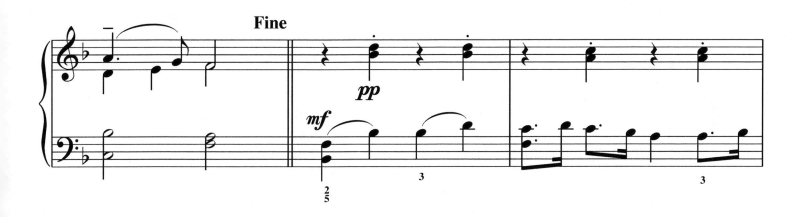

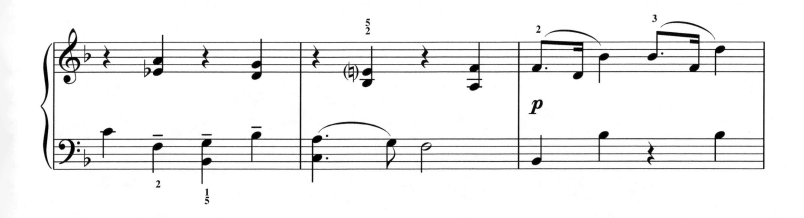

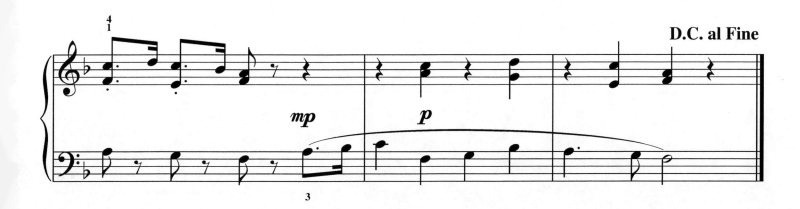

Havah Nagilah

Traditional Israeli Folk Song

Vigorous

Fine

Faster

accel.

rit.

D.C. al Fine

Matty Groves

Traditional English Folk Song

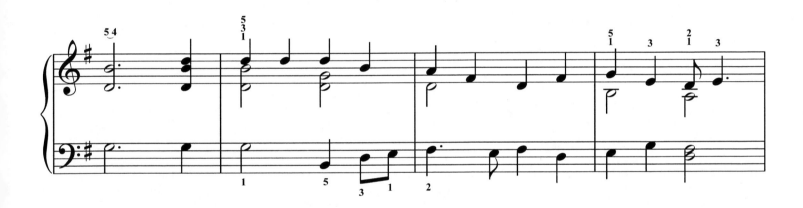

Kalinka

Traditional Russian Folk Song

Begin slowly, then gradually get faster

D.S. al Coda

Coda

Little Brown Jug

Traditional American Folk Song

Moderately

Londonderry Air

Traditional Irish Air

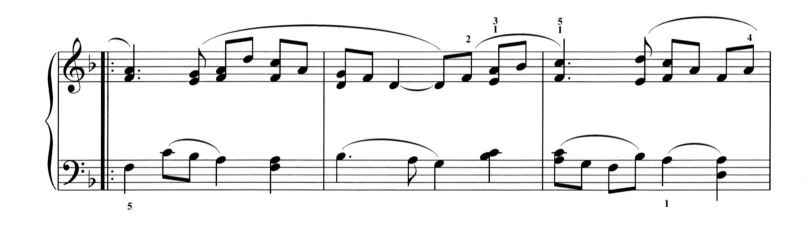

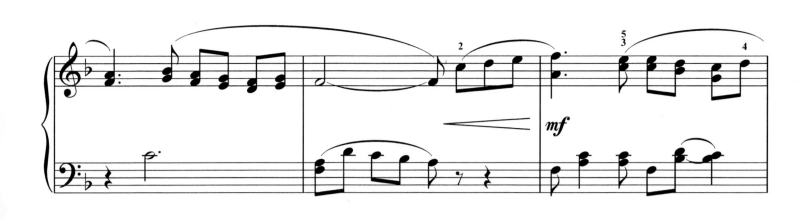

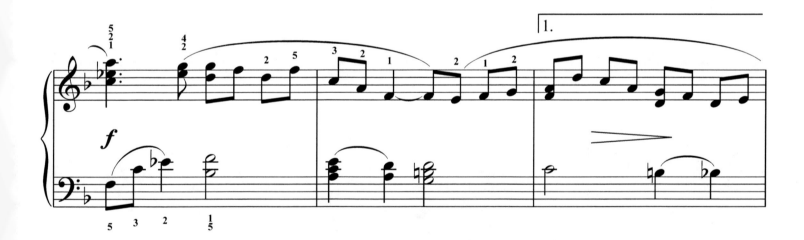

The Minstrel Boy

Traditional Irish Folk Song

My Bonnie Lies Over The Ocean

Traditional Scottish Folk Song

Smoothly

Oh! Susanna

American Folk Song
by Stephen Foster

25

Santa Lucia

Neapolitan Song
by Teodoro Cottrau

She Moved Through The Fair

Traditional Irish Folk Song

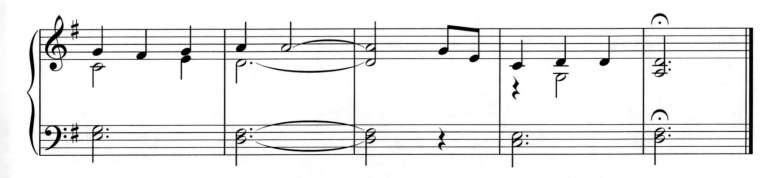

Simple Gifts

Traditional American Shaker Hymn

Bright, but steadily

dim.

mp

f

Slower

rit.

29

Skye Boat Song

Traditional Scottish Folk Song

Waltzing Matilda

Australian Folk Song
by Marie Cowan

1 2 3 4 5 6 7 8 9